Gym Scooter
Fun & Games

Guy Bailey

EP

EDUCATORS PRESS

Vancouver, Washington

ISBN: 978-0-9669727-7-1

Publisher's Cataloging-in-Publication
(Provided by Quality Books, Inc.)

Bailey, Guy, 1956-
Gym scooter fun & games / Guy Bailey.
p. cm.
Includes index.
LCCN 2006907695
ISBN-13: 978-0-9669727-7-1
ISBN-10: 0-9669-7277-5

1. Physical education for children--Study and
teaching (Elementary)--Activity programs. 2. Sports for
children--Study and teaching (Elementary)--Activity
programs. 3. Games.   I. Title.

GV443.B2615 2007   372.86'044
                          QBI06-600349

The author and publisher assume that the reader will teach these games using professional judgment and respect for
student safety. In regards to this statement, the author and publisher shall have neither liability nor responsibility in the
case of injury to anyone participating in the activities contained within.

EDUCATORS PRESS
15610 NE 2nd Street
Vancouver, WA 98684
(360) 597-4355
www.educatorspress.com

Printed in the United States of America

Contents

Acknowledgments

Many thanks go out to all my colleagues in the physical education profession. Because some of the game ideas contained in this resource have been collected from attending workshops and conventions for over two decades, it is impossible to give specific game credit. However, I have learned so much from you in our sharing of ideas and teaching methodology over the years. Your professional advice and enthusiasm for a book of this type is much appreciated. Thanks also to the American Alliance for Health, Physical Education, Recreation, and Dance (AAHPERD), the National Association for Sport and Physical Education (NASPE), the Canadian Association for Health, Physical Education, and Dance (CAHPERD), and the Australian Council for Health, Physical Education, and Recreation, Inc. (ACHPER) for your outstanding leadership and professional guidance.

Special thanks to the wonderful students at Mill Plain Elementary School in Vancouver, Washington who voluntarily played many of these games. I would have had few opportunities to try, modify, and create these game ideas without them. Their exuberance for scooter play was a constant source of inspiration and encouragement.

I would also like to acknowledge the many talented professionals that contributed to the design and production of this book. I am particularly indebted to Olga Melnik for her outstanding diagrams and illustrations. The setup and play procedures of each game in this book is made easier because of her gift at making games come "alive" for readers. I would also like to single out Gerald Bergstrom for his masterful front and back cover design.

Finally, an author's family is always owed the greatest amount of gratitude, for they're the ones who make the biggest sacrifices. A special "Thank you!" goes out to each of my four children—Justin, Austin, Heather, and Carson—for their understanding, encouragement, and support.

Preface

The idea for this book actually came about several years ago while preparing a series of physical education lessons that called for the use of gym scooters. In my planning, I quickly realized that most physical education books contain very little information, if any at all, about the use of gym scooters. In fact, after an exhaustive search, I could not find a single resource that focused entirely on gym scooter games and activities. As a consequence, I started compiling a lengthy list of gym scooter activities and games that developed specific learning objectives, proved to be safe, and were fun. Along the way, I modified many of these games to better meet the needs of my students, and created completely new games as well. *Gym Scooter Fun & Games* is the result of that work.

In all, more than 80 games and scooter movement activities are included to meet the needs of a wide variety of student ages in a physical education or recreational setting. There are games for both large and small groups, sport lead-up games, relay activities, tag-type games, and games that call for the use of scooters in combination with other equipment. In choosing the activities for this book, I purposely left out those that take an excessive amount of time to set up and/or explain to students. It's my philosophy that the more time kids are physically active in physical education—the better.

Each activity provides everything needed for its successful use. This includes an introduction, easy-to-understand directions, grade level suggestions, number of participants required, and equipment needed. Also included are helpful diagrams and illustrations to help you visualize the set-up procedures. In addition, you will find information on how to use gym scooters safely in a physical education setting.

Although *Gym Scooter Fun & Games* is an ideal supplement to a broad-based physical education, it is by no means intended to a complete curriculum. Its purpose is to supply you with wide assortment of gym scooter activities that can develop specific motor/cognitive skills and strengthen student interest in physical activity. Ultimately, it's my desire that these activities will help vitalize your physical education program—leaving you with enthusiastic students who crave movement and game playing.

It's also my hope that this book will inspire all of you to revive those underused gym scooters. If you have never used gym scooters, I would encourage you to buy a full classroom set today from your favorite physical education catalog and introduce these exciting activities to your students. As you'll discover, the usage of gym scooters is virtually unlimited and can serve physical educators in a variety of diverse situations.

I trust you'll find *Gym Scooter Fun & Games* to be a much-used resource and a valuable addition to your professional library. Have fun!

Gym Scooter
"Rules of the Road"

Safety is a primary consideration when using gym scooters. As important to giving students the directions of how to play a game, leaders need to also routinely teach the rules of safe play with each activity. The following suggestions will significantly reduce the potential of accidents and injuries:

Rule #1: Never allow students to stand on the scooter.

Rule #2: Remind students to keep fingers, hair, and clothing away from the wheels of the scooter.

Rule #3: Remind students to always position the body squarely on the scooter. The scooter can tip if one's body placement is off-balance.

Rule #4: Scooter handles are not really "handles," and are not meant to be held on to. Instead, think of them as "bumpers." Hands should be safely enclosed *inside*. In this way, hands and fingers are not exposed.

Rule #5: When working with a partner, remind the partner applying the movement force that he or she is *responsible* for the safety of the partner on the scooter. Enforce speed limits!

Rule #6: When pushing a partner, get low and push the partner's lower back. Do *not* place hands on the shoulders and push unless the student being pushed is using two scooters for support. In addition, it is a good idea to always pair up partners of similar size.

Rule #7: When conducting relays, remind the students to always keep their eyes up, facing forward, (not down). Provide plenty of spacing between lanes.

Rule #8: Never allow students to let go of a scooter—with or without a passenger—to create a flying missile.

Rule #9: As with driving a car, reinforce the importance of proper spacing while moving on a scooter among other "drivers." Besides the possibility of bumping/crashing into other scooters, a player's hands, fingers, and hair can be injured by the wheels of close-by scooters.

Rule #10: Having the students stop immediately when a signal is given can help assure safety (the whistle works great in a high-noise environment). Create a "stop-and-listen" routine in which students quickly stop, turn their scooter upside down, and sit on the floor beside their scooter in a pretzel position.

Relay Challenges

Single Scooter Relays

SKILLS/OBJECTIVES: Cooperative play, upper-lower body coordination, motor skills, team work

NUMBER OF PLAYERS: Arrange the players into equal teams of 2-4 players each

EQUIPMENT: One scooter for each team; two cones per team

HOW TO PLAY: Before the introduction of relays, it's important to allow students a sufficient amount of individual practice time with the required tasks. Give each child a scooter and challenge the players to try the tasks listed below on their own. In addition, use this practice time to go over important safety guidelines (see page 7).

Divide the players into equal teams. Use the cones to mark out a starting line and a turning line that are about 30 feet apart. This distance can be adjusted according to the age of the players and the level of difficulty related to the movement task.

On a starting signal, the first player on each team performs the required movement task all the way around the turning cone and back. The next teammate in line then takes the scooter and performs the same task with the previous performer going to the back of the line. This rotation continues until each team member has performed the movement task. The objective is to be the first team to fully complete the movement task.

The following are single scooter tasks that can be used as relays:

Seated Relay

The players sit on their bottoms with their hands gripping the handles or sides of the scooter. They can sit backwards and push forward with their feet, or sit facing forward and propel themselves by "walking" in a forward direction with their feet.

Lying Relay

The players lie face down with the scooter under the middle of the body. The legs are straightened out and do not touch the floor. Players propel themselves forward using the arms/hands in a "breaststroke" swimming motion.

Kneeling Relay

Players kneel on the scooter and move forward using the hands only.

Alligator Crawl

The player lie face down with the scooter under the middle of the body (much like the Lying Relay above). Imitating the movement of an alligator, players push with their feet and pull with their hands.

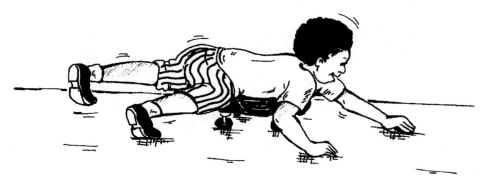

Pretzel Relay

Players sit with legs crossed on a scooter. They propel themselves forward with their hands out to the side.

Bear Scoot Relay

With both hands, players grip the handles or sides of the scooter and run forward. For safety reasons, emphasize that their head should be up and eyes facing forward. In addition, make sure there is adequate spacing between the teams.

Street Scooter Relay

This task resembles the movement required in propelling a common street scooter—except there's no standing. The players place both hands and one knee on the scooter. With the other leg out to the side, they propel themselves forward with their foot.

Walrus Relay

This relay is great for developing upper body strength! The players begin by placing their shins or feet on top of the scooter, and then move forward with the hands until they are in a push-up position. Using their hands (with the arms in a locked position), they move forward dragging their scooter behind them.

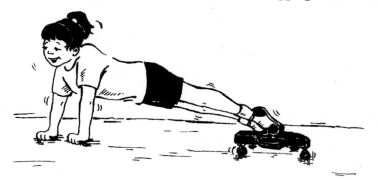

One-Hand Relay

Players place one hand on the scooter (in the middle), and run forward. Have them change hands as they pass the turning cone. For safety reasons, emphasize that their head should be up and eyes facing forward. In addition, make sure there is adequate spacing between the teams.

Kangaroo Relay

Players place both hands on the scooter, and lift one foot off the ground. They propel themselves forward with the other foot (in a hopping motion). Have them change legs as they pass the turning cone. As with many of the previous relays, all players should have their heads up and eyes forward when moving.

Crab Walk Relay

This relay imitates the regular crab walk. However, it is quite strenuous and the required traveling distance should be shortened. Players begin in a crab position (that is, stomachs facing upward and bottoms off the floor) with their feet on top of the scooter. Using their hands, they crab walk forward or backward.

Partner Scooter Relays

SKILLS/OBJECTIVES: Cooperative play, upper-lower body coordination, motor skills, team work

NUMBER OF PLAYERS: Arrange the players into pairs

EQUIPMENT: One scooter (or two scooters depending on the specific relay) and two cones for each team

HOW TO PLAY: Before introducing partner relays to your students, it's important to allow a sufficient amount of free practice time with the various required tasks.

Divide the players into pairs. Use the cones to mark out a starting line and a turning line that are about 30 feet apart. This distance can be adjusted according to the age of the students and the level of difficulty related to the movement task.

On a starting signal, the first player on each team performs the required movement task all the way around the turning cone and back. The next teammate in line then takes the scooter and performs the same task with the previous performer going to the back of the line. This rotation continues until each team member has performed the task. The objective is to be the first team to fully complete the movement task.

The following are partner scooter tasks that be used as relays:

Siamese Twins Relay

Players sit on their scooters next to their partner side-by-side. Have each pair link elbows and/or grab their partner's inside scooter handle. Players use their feet to travel.

Back-to-Back Relay

Each player, while sitting on a scooter, goes back-to-back with a partner with the elbows linked. The partners travel by having the player going forward pulling with the feet and the player going backward pushing with the feet.

Pushcart Relay

One player sits on one scooter and places his/her feet on the other scooter. The partner places his/her hands on the partner's upper back and pushes the "cart" forward.

Wheelbarrow Relay

One partner places his/her hands on a scooter and gets into a "push-up" position. The other partner grabs the feet, lifts the legs, and pushes the "wheelbarrow" forward.

Horse & Cart Relay

This relay is performed somewhat like the pushcart relay above. However, instead of pushing, the "horse" partner now is pulling with a jump rope that is positioned around the waist. The seated partner holds the ends of the rope (like horse reins).

Medic Relay

One player lies facing up on two scooters. The partner picks up the legs by grabbing the feet, and pulls the "ambulance" backward.

Jet Relay

One player lies on both scooters face down with outstretched arms to the sides, resembling a "jet." The partner places his/her hands on the back and pushes the Jet forward. The Jet can also help in moving forward by using the two wings (that is, the outstretched hands).

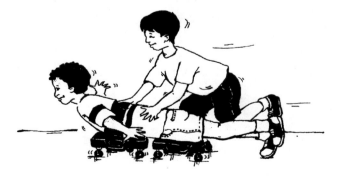

Link Relay

All players, while sitting on their scooters, face their partner and place their feet in each other's lap. They then both lean backwards, and propel themselves forward or backward, using only their hands.

Tag Games

Scooter Tag

SKILLS/OBJECTIVES: Scooter skills, cardiovascular fitness

NUMBER OF PLAYERS: Unlimited

EQUIPMENT: One scooter for each player; three foam balls

HOW TO PLAY: All players begin seated on scooters. Choose several players to be "It." The Its start in the middle of the play area and each has a foam ball in hand for tagging. The other players scatter throughout the play area.

On a starting signal, the Its try to tag the free players by touching them with the ball (no throwing allowed). If touched by the ball, a player is immediately frozen at that spot, and must extend his or her arms outward while remaining seated on the scooter. Another player can free the frozen player by passing under the extended arms.

The objective is to avoid getting tagged for as long as possible.

Scooter Germ Tag

SKILLS/OBJECTIVES: Scooter skills, cardiovascular fitness

NUMBER OF PLAYERS: Unlimited

EQUIPMENT: One scooter for each player; four foam balls

HOW TO PLAY: All players begin seated on their scooters. Choose several players to be "IT." The Its start in the middle of the play area and each has a foam ball (the "germs") in hand. All of the other players scatter around the play area.

On a starting signal, the Its try to tag a free player by touching him or her with the "germ". Once tagged, that player is now stuck with the germ and the only way to get rid of it is to tag another player. At no time are the Its allowed to throw the ball.

The objective is to avoid getting tagged (that is, stuck with the "germ"). Play until time is called.

Scooter Switch Tag

SKILLS/OBJECTIVES: Scooter skills, cardiovascular fitness

NUMBER OF PLAYERS: Unlimited

EQUIPMENT: One scooter for each player; if possible, use only two colors of scooters

HOW TO PLAY: This vigorous game is perfect as a warm-up activity in physical education. If possible, each player should have a scooter that is one of two colors. Designate one color of scooters to be the "Its." If you must play with several different-colored scooters, then pick the color you have the most of to start out as the Its.

On a starting signal, the Its move around and chase the other players. For example, if the blue colored scooters are designated as the Its, then all the players seated on blue scooters attempt to tag the players seated on the non-blue scooters. When a player on a blue scooter tags a player on a different-colored scooter, they switch scooters and the new player on the blue scooter becomes an It. The new It cannot tag the player who just tagged him. Play is continuous.

Scooter Snakes

SKILLS/OBJECTIVES: Scooter skills, cardiovascular fitness

NUMBER OF PLAYERS: Unlimited

EQUIPMENT: One scooter for each player; 20-30 pool noodles

HOW TO PLAY: This fun game calls for the use of pool noodles. They can be found in most physical education catalogs or sporting supply stores.

All players begin seated on scooters. Choose several players to be the "Snakes," and hand each a noodle for tagging. The other players scatter throughout the play area.

On a starting signal, the Snakes try to tag the free players by touching them with the noodle (or "fangs"). If touched, a player must grab the spot where he or she was "bitten," and keep playing. When touched with a noodle a second time, the player uses the other hand to cover the spot of the "bite," and continues playing. When "bitten" a third time, the player takes a noodle from the game leader and becomes an It (or Snake). The number of Snakes will continue to grow throughout the game. The objective is to avoid getting tagged for as long as possible.

Scooter Bridge Tag

SKILLS/OBJECTIVES: Cardiovascular fitness, agility

NUMBER OF PLAYERS: Unlimited

EQUIPMENT: One scooter for each player; three foam balls

HOW TO PLAY: All players begin seated on scooters. Choose several players to be "It." The Its start in the middle of the play area and each has a foam ball in hand for tagging. The other players scatter throughout the play area.

On a starting signal, the Its try to tag the free players by touching them with the ball (no throwing allowed). If touched, a player is immediately frozen at that spot, and must raise his or her arm upward while remaining seated on the scooter. The frozen player can be freed only by having two players team up by facing each other, hands placed on the floor behind their scooters for support, legs raised with the bottoms of the feet touching (forming a "bridge"), allowing the frozen player to travel underneath on his or her scooter. Its are not allowed to tag players who are in the process of forming bridges.

The objective is to avoid getting tagged for as long as possible.

24

Scooter Maniacs

SKILLS/OBJECTIVES: Scooter skills, cardiovascular fitness

NUMBER OF PLAYERS: Unlimited

EQUIPMENT: One scooter for each player; enough foam balls for each player

HOW TO PLAY: All players begin seated on scooters. Choose one player to start out as the "Maniac." He or she starts in the middle of the play area with a small foam ball. The other players scatter throughout the play area. A box of small foam balls is set in the middle of the play area.

On a starting signal, the Maniac pursues the other players and attempts to touch them with the ball. No throwing is allowed. If touched, a player goes to the box of foam balls, takes one out, and becomes a maniac (or "helper') too. The number of maniacs will grow throughout the game. The game ends when just one free player is left in the game.

Scooter Chain Tag

SKILLS/OBJECTIVES: Scooter skills, cardiovascular fitness

NUMBER OF PLAYERS: Unlimited

EQUIPMENT: One scooter for each player

HOW TO PLAY: All players begin seated on scooters. Choose one player to start out as the "It." The other players scatter throughout the play area.

On a starting signal, the It moves after the other players and attempts to tag someone. Once tagged, a player "connects" to the It by locking inside arms or grabbing each other's scooter handles, and then the two players attempt to tag a third player, a fourth, and so on. This process continues until there is a complete chain. Once connected to the chain, players cannot let go. Play continues until the last free player is tagged.

Scooter Blob Tag

SKILLS/OBJECTIVES: Scooter skills, cardiovascular fitness

NUMBER OF PLAYERS: Unlimited

EQUIPMENT: One scooter for each player

HOW TO PLAY: All players begin seated on scooters. Choose two players to make the "Blob." To make the Blob, the two players lock inside arms or grab each other's scooter handles. The other players scatter throughout the play area.

   The game begins with the Blob moving around trying to tag the other participants. Once tagged, a player joins the Blob by locking inside arms or grabbing each other's scooter handles. When the group of three manages to tag another player, instead of making a line of four (as in Scooter Chain Tag), they separate into two pairs. The game continues in this pattern of growing and dividing until all of the participants have been tagged.

Scooter Foot Tag

SKILLS/OBJECTIVES: Cardiovascular fitness, agility, coordination

NUMBER OF PLAYERS: Unlimited

EQUIPMENT: One scooter for each player; several small foam balls

HOW TO PLAY: All players begin by lying on scooters with legs extended. Choose several players to be "It." The Its start in the middle of the play area, lying on scooters, and each has a foam ball in hand for tagging. The other players scatter throughout the play area.

On a starting signal, the Its move around on their scooters trying to tag the free players by touching them with the ball on a foot. No throwing is allowed. Once tagged, that player takes the ball and becomes an It. The objective is to avoid getting tagged for as long as possible. Players are not allowed to travel any way other than on lying on their stomachs.

Since the Its are always changing, the game is played non-stop. Play until time is called.

VARIATION: Consider pairing the students and play using a one-on-one format.

Sport Games

Garbage Basketball

SKILLS/OBJECTIVES: Basketball passing, catching, shooting, team work, cooperation

NUMBER OF PLAYERS: Arrange the players into two equal teams of 5 players each; for large groups, set up additional play areas and play multiple games simultaneously

EQUIPMENT: One scooter for each player; one basketball, different colored jerseys for each team, two garbage cans or cardboard boxes, floor tape

HOW TO PLAY: Divide the players into two teams of five players each. Place the two garbage cans or cardboard boxes in the middle of each end of the rectangular play area (or the regular basketball court) for the "goals." Using floor tape, mark a 6-8 foot circle around each goal to represent the restraining lines. The players position themselves as if playing basketball and all must be seated on scooters.

 Garbage Basketball is played with many of the rules and strategies of regular basketball. However, the object of this game is to score a goal by shooting the basketball into the opponent's container. To begin, designate one team to start first on offense. The offensive team passes the basketball inbounds from its end line, and attempts to advance the ball down the court by passing and dribbling. A player can scoot with the ball for up to five seconds before he/she must pass or shoot. Offensive players can only shoot from outside the 6-8 foot restraining lines that circle the "hoops." Because the game is played indoors, the walls can be used for passing or shooting.

 Defensive players can attempt to intercept passes, steal the ball from dribblers, and can pick up any free ball while it is on the floor. However, like basketball, no defensive player can make contact with an offensive player.

 After each score, the non-scoring team passes the ball inbounds from behind its end line and play resumes.

Scooter Basketball

SKILLS/OBJECTIVES: Basketball skills, cooperation, team work

NUMBER OF PLAYERS: Arrange the players into two equal teams of 5 players each; for large groups, set up additional play areas and play multiple games simultaneously

EQUIPMENT: One scooter for each player; one basketball, different colored jerseys for each game

HOW TO PLAY: *Scooter Basketball* is played much like *Garbage Basketball* (see previous game), but now players are attempting to score by shooting at regular basketball goals. Because the players are seated on scooters, it is highly recommended that the basketball goals be lowered to 8 feet and/or the game restricted to students in the middle school grades.

The game is played on a regular basketball court. Position the players into basketball positions, with all seated on scooters. Rather than a jump ball, the game begins with one team starting with the ball by their end line. The objective of the offensive team is to advance the basketball down the court by dribbling and passing, and score by shooting the ball into the opponent's hoop. "Traveling" is called if a player scoots for more than 5 seconds without passing or dribbling. Because the game is played indoors, the walls can be used for passing.

Defensive players can intercept passes, block shots, and steal the ball at anytime. However, no touching or contact with an offensive player is allowed.

After each score, the non-scoring team resumes play by passing the ball in from behind the end line.

Arena Scooter Football

SKILLS/OBJECTIVES: Football passing, receiving, team work

NUMBER OF PLAYERS: Arrange the players into two equal teams of 4-6 players each; for large groups, set up additional play areas and play multiple games simultaneously

EQUIPMENT: One scooter for each player; one foam football, cone markers, different colored jerseys for each team

HOW TO PLAY: *Arena Scooter Football* is a modified version of Flag Football. In this game, the objective is to score a touchdown by crossing the opponent's goal line with the football (while seated on a scooter) before the completion of four downs.

Using cone markers, designate two end zones in the gymnasium. Form two equal-sized teams of 4-6 players, with each player seated on a scooter. For large-size classes, set up two game areas by playing sideways on the two half courts.

Designate one team to start the game on offense. The offensive team must select one player to be the quarterback (the others are pass receivers). Since there are no kickoffs, the offensive team begins play on its own goal line with the quarterback holding the football. On "Hike," the offensive receivers go down the court to catch a pass from the quarterback. If completed, the receiver continues to scoot toward the opponent's goal line until tackled with a two-hand touch. The next play begins from there. If a pass is incomplete, the ball goes back to the original line-of-scrimmage. In all, the offense has four downs to score a touchdown (worth 6 points).

Arena Scooter Football (continued)

The defensive players, as in flag football, cannot touch a receiver prior to the ball arriving. However, they are allowed to intercept passes. After each score or four downs, the ball is given the other team and they now have a chance to play offense from their goal line.

This is strictly a passing game. There are no handoffs, and the quarterback cannot scoot pass the line-of-scrimmage during a play.

Ultimate Scooter Football

SKILLS/OBJECTIVES: Football passing, receiving, team work

NUMBER OF PLAYERS: Arrange the players into two equal teams

EQUIPMENT: One scooter for each player; one foam football, cone markers, different colored jerseys for each team

HOW TO PLAY: *Ultimate Scooter Football* is an indoor scooter adaptation of Ultimate Frisbee, a popular outdoor game.

Using the cone markers, designate two end zones in the gym. Divide the class into two equal teams, each wearing different colored jerseys. Each team is assigned an end zone to defend. The two teams start at their own end zones, with each player seated on a scooter. Since there is no kickoff, the game leader selects one team to start on offense.

The team chosen to begin first on offense starts the game by advancing the football down the court with passes. The objective is to eventually have a teammate catch the football in the end zone for a touchdown (worth 6 points). A player in possession of the football cannot move, and has up to five seconds to pass it to a teammate. A pass can be made forward, backward, or sideways to a teammate. However, once a pass hits the ground or is dropped, a "turnover" is committed and the other team takes possession of the ball at that spot.

Defensive players may intercept a pass at any time, but are not allowed to take it away from the hands of the offensive player.

After each touchdown, the non-scoring team begins with the football on their goal line and play resumes.

VARIATION: Consider playing with two or more football at the same time, especially with a large-size class.

Scooter End Zone

SKILLS/OBJECTIVES: Football passing, receiving, team work

NUMBER OF PLAYERS: Arrange the players into two equal teams

EQUIPMENT: One scooter for each player; two or more foam footballs, cone markers

HOW TO PLAY: *Scooter End Zone* is a scooter version of End Zone, a popular football lead-up game.

Using the cone markers, designate two end zones in the gym. A center line divides the play area into two halves. Divide the class into two equal teams. Each team has half of its players located in an end zone and half in the court area opposite the center line. Each of the four groups must stay within its boundaries throughout the game. All players are seated on scooters. One player on each team starts with a foam football in hand.

The game begins with the two players in possession of the football throwing to teammates in the end zones. The objective is to have a teammate in the end zone catch the passed ball for a score (worth one point). Whether successful or not, the end zone players return the football to their teammates in the court area with a pass (no kicking allowed) and play continues non-stop.

At halftime, have the end zone players switch with their teammates in the court areas. Periodically, add more footballs to the game.

At the end of play, the team with the highest number of points wins the game.

Knock Down Hockey

SKILLS/OBJECTIVES: Hockey striking, cardiovascular fitness, scooter skills

NUMBER OF PLAYERS: Unlimited; arrange the players into two equal teams.

EQUIPMENT: One scooter, one short hockey stick, one plastic puck, and protective eyeglasses for each player; 20-50 lightweight plastic bowling pins

HOW TO PLAY: This high energy game utilizes the short hockey sticks and protective eyeglasses available in most physical education catalogs.

In a gymnasium, place the plastic bowling pins randomly throughout the playing area, with all of them standing. Divide the class into two equal teams. Each team lines up along a designated sideline, with each player sitting on a scooter, eyeglasses on, and a short hockey stick and puck in hand. To begin, one team will start out as the "strikers," and the other as the "set'em uppers."

On a starting signal, the striking team quickly scoots around and attempts to strike their puck at the bowling pins with the objective of knocking over as many as possible. Meanwhile, the other team leaves their sticks and pucks on their sideline, scoots out into the play area and sets up as many downed pins as possible. At the end of one minute, the group that has more pins in their desired position (standing or knocked over) is the winner. Have the teams change roles and repeat the game.

Caution the strikers that they cannot knock over any pins with their hands or sticks—only a moving puck counts. Also, the team setting up the pins cannot interfere or block any of the strikers from knocking over the pins.

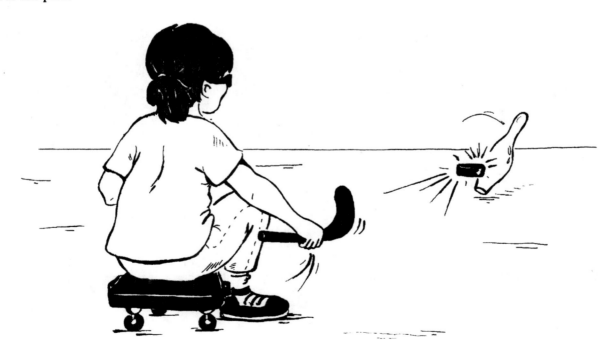

Scooter Pirates

SKILLS/OBJECTIVES: Scooter skills, hockey skills, cardiovascular fitness

NUMBER OF PLAYERS: Unlimited

EQUIPMENT: One scooter, one short hockey stick, and protective eyeglasses for each player; enough pucks for half the class

HOW TO PLAY: *Scooter Hockey Pirates* is a terrific game for developing puck handling, stealing, and scooter agility. Using the lines of a basketball court, place half of the class on a sideline with each player seated on a scooter and a short hockey stick in hand (these players are the "Pirates"). The other half of the class is seated on scooters throughout the play area with each player having a hockey stick and puck.

On a starting signal, the Pirates (that is, the players on the sideline without pucks) chase the other players (who have pucks) and attempt to steal away their pucks. Once a player loses his or her puck to a pirate, then that player becomes a pirate and the former pirate now possesses the puck. The new pirate cannot steal a puck from the player who just his or her puck.

At no time can players use their free hand to steal a puck or to prevent Pirates from stealing. Players must remain seated on their scooters throughout the game.

Mini Scooter Hockey

SKILLS/OBJECTIVES: Hockey striking, goalie play, scooter movement, team work

NUMBER OF PLAYERS: Arrange the players into two teams of 3 players each. For large groups, set up additional play areas and multiple games simultaneously

EQUIPMENT: One scooter, one short hockey stick and protective eyeglasses for each player; one plastic puck, two hockey goals (or substitute tumbling mats that are set upright) for each game, floor tape

HOW TO PLAY: This 3-on-3 game, a modification of floor hockey, utilizes the short hockey sticks available in most physical education catalogs. Protective eyeglasses can also be found in most catalogs.

Using a basketball court, set up several play areas by placing the goals on the side lines (should have enough space for 3 or 4 play areas). Using floor tape, mark off a 4-6 foot restraining line around each goal.

Each team has a goalie, who stops shots using the hands, feet, or stick; and two forwards, who work together to score.

Play is exactly like regular floor hockey, with the following exceptions:
- Players cannot swing their sticks above waist level (and, remember, they're sitting on scooters)
- Players cannot advance the puck with their feet or hands
- At no time are players allowed to leave their scooter
- Since the walls are not utilized as boundaries, players are free to roam anywhere. However, scores can only be made by hitting the puck into the goal from inside the play area.

The objective is to hit the puck into the opponent's goal for a score (worth one point). After each score, the puck is placed in the middle of the court and the two rovers have a face-off.

Scooter Hockey Duel

SKILLS/OBJECTIVES: Hockey striking, goalie play, scooter movement

NUMBER OF PLAYERS: Arrange the players into pairs. For large groups, set up additional play areas and multiple games simultaneously

EQUIPMENT: One scooter, one short hockey stick and protective eyeglasses for each player; one plastic puck, two cones for each game

HOW TO PLAY: This one-on-one game, a modification of floor hockey, utilizes the short hockey sticks available in most physical education catalogs. Protective eyeglasses can also be found in most catalogs.

Set up multiple play areas around the gymnasium by placing two cones about 20-30 feet apart (to represent the goals). Assign two players to a play area.

The two players begin with a "face-off" in the middle of the two cones. The objective is to control the puck and drive toward the opponent's cone in order to shoot and hit it for a score (worth one point). Play is exactly like regular floor hockey, with the following exceptions:

- Players cannot swing their sticks above waist level (and, remember, they're sitting on scooters)
- Players cannot advance the puck with their feet or hands
- At no time are players allowed to leave their scooter
- Since the walls are not utilized as boundaries, players are free to roam anywhere.

After each score, the puck is placed in the middle of the play area and the two players have a face-off.

Scooter Hockey

SKILLS/OBJECTIVES: Hockey striking, goalie play, scooter movement, team work

NUMBER OF PLAYERS: Arrange the players into two teams of 6 players each. For large groups, set up additional play areas and multiple games simultaneously

EQUIPMENT: One scooter, one short hockey stick and protective eyeglasses for each player; one plastic puck, two hockey goals (or substitute tumbling mats that are set upright), floor tape

HOW TO PLAY: The game of *Scooter Hockey*, a modification of regular floor hockey, utilizes the short hockey sticks available in most physical education catalogs. Protective eyeglasses can also be found in most catalogs.

In a gymnasium, set up two hockey goals at opposite ends. Using floor tape, mark off a 4-6 foot restraining line around each goal. The walls can serve as boundaries.

   Each team has a goalie, who stops shots using the hands, feet, or stick; a rover, who is the only player allowed to roam the full court; two guards, who play defense and are not allowed to cross the center line; and two forwards, who work together with the rover to score but cannot cross the center line to the defensive side.

Scooter Hockey (continued)

Play is exactly like regular floor hockey, with the following exceptions:
- Players cannot swing their sticks above waist level (and, remember, they're sitting on scooters)
- Players cannot advance the puck with their feet or hands
- At no time are players allowed to leave their scooter

The objective is to hit the puck into the opponent's goal for a score (worth one point). After each score, the puck is placed in the middle of the court and the two rovers have a face-off.

Four Goal Scooter Hockey

SKILLS/OBJECTIVES: Hockey striking, goalie play, scooter movement, team work

NUMBER OF PLAYERS: Unlimited; arrange the players into two equal teams.

EQUIPMENT: One scooter, one short hockey stick and protective eyeglasses for each player; several plastic puck, four hockey goals (or use tumbling mats that are set upright), floor tape

HOW TO PLAY: The game of *Four Goal Scooter Hockey*, a modification of regular floor hockey, utilizes the short hockey sticks available in most physical education catalogs. Protective eyeglasses can also be found in most catalogs. This is a great activity for increasing your students' opportunities to score and play goalie.

In a gymnasium, set up a hockey goal at each end and along both sides (in all, a total of four goals). Using floor tape, mark off a 4-6 foot restraining line around each goal. The walls can serve as boundaries.

Divide the class into two equal teams. Each team has two goalies. The other players are "rovers," who are free to roam anywhere around the court. All players start in a sitting position on their scooters.

To begin, the game instructor drops a puck in the middle of the play area. Players from both teams attempt to gain control of the puck and score at either of the opponent's goals. After a score, the goalie simply rolls the puck toward the middle of the court and play continues nonstop. Add additional pucks every few minutes. Play is exactly like regular floor hockey, with the following exceptions:

Players cannot swing their sticks above waist level (and, remember, they're sitting on scooters). In addition, players must remain on their scooters at all times.

Scooter Soccer

SKILLS/OBJECTIVES: Soccer kicking, heading, trapping, goalie play, team work

NUMBER OF PLAYERS: Arrange the players into two equal teams of 6 players each; for large groups, set up additional play areas and play multiple games simultaneously

EQUIPMENT: One scooter for each player; one foam soccer ball, two soccer nets (or substitute cones) for each game

HOW TO PLAY: Scooter Soccer is best played in a gymnasium, with the walls serving as boundaries. Place a net at both ends for the goals and mark a restraining line about 6 feet around each goal. Form two teams of six players. Each team has three forwards, two halfbacks, and one goalie. Have the players get into position, seated on their scooters, forwards lined up and facing each other.

As in regular soccer, the game begins with a kickoff. The objective is to gain possession of the ball, advance it down the court (without using the hands or arms), and score by kicking the ball into the opponent's goal. Each player must stay on his/her scooter at all times. Players can only make contact with the ball with the head, feet, legs, and torso (with the exception of the goalies, who are allowed to use hands). There are no out of bounds (players simply play the ball off the wall).

A team receives one point for each goal. After each score, the ball is placed in the middle of the play area and the non-scoring team kicks off to restart the game.

VARIATION: Consider adding additional balls. After a score, the goalie retrieves the ball out of the net, kicks the ball toward a teammate, and play continues non-stop.

Bull In The Ring

SKILLS/OBJECTIVES: Soccer dribbling, cardiovascular fitness

NUMBER OF PLAYERS: 3-4 players to a game; set up multiple play areas for larger groups

EQUIPMENT: One scooter for each game; one soccer ball for each player; floor tape for marking the circle

HOW TO PLAY: This fun game develops soccer dribbling/ball control skills, and can used as an entire class activity (multiple games played simultaneously) or as part of a soccer station lesson.

With the floor tape, mark off a circle that is about 15 feet in diameter. For large-size groups, set up multiple play areas and play several games simultaneously. One player (the "Bull") sits on a scooter inside the circle. The other players (the "dribblers") stand anywhere inside the circle with a foot on top of their ball.

The dribblers' objective is to last as long as possible without getting "tagged" by the Bull (the player on the scooter). On a starting signal, the Bull moves around on the scooter and attempts to kick a dribbler's soccer ball outside the circle with his or her feet (no hands allowed). If successful, the Bull retrieves the ball, runs back to the circle, and becomes a dribbler. Meanwhile, the player who lost his or her ball immediately sits down on the scooter and becomes the new Bull. Any dribbler who accidentally kicks his or her ball outside the circle becomes the new Bull, regardless whether the Bull actually touched the ball or not. Play continues in this fashion until time is called.

Scooter Diamond Ball

SKILLS/OBJECTIVES: Rolling, throwing, catching, softball knowledge, team work

NUMBER OF PLAYERS: Arrange the players into two equal teams

EQUIPMENT: One scooter for each player; one foam soccer-size ball, floor tape to mark the four bases for each game

HOW TO PLAY: *Scooter Diamond Ball* is a variation of kickball (using mostly softball rules) and, of course, it's played indoors on scooters. Set up the bases as a softball diamond, with home plate and the three bases all spaced about 30 feet apart (floor tape works best). Form two equal teams, with one team in regular softball fielding positions and the other team standing in a file formation ready to bat. The pitcher begins the game holding a soccer-size foam ball. The defensive players, as well as the batter, must be seated on their scooters.

As in kickball, the pitcher begins by rolling the ball toward the batter at home plate. The batter can kick the ball, strike it with a fist, or catch and then throw it out into fair territory. The rules of softball apply with base running, outs, scoring, etc., with one exception—all players must move about on scooters. In addition, because this game is played indoors, all walls are in play.

A team receives one point (or "run") for each offensive player who successfully gets back to home plate.

VARIATION: Instead of three outs, consider having the teams switch after each member of the batting team has had a chance at batting.

45

Scooter Scoop Softball

SKILLS/OBJECTIVES: Lacrosse-type skills (throwing and catching with plastic scoops and balls), softball knowledge, team work

NUMBER OF PLAYERS: Arrange the players into two equal teams

EQUIPMENT: One scooter and plastic scoop for each player; one whiffle ball, floor tape to mark the four bases for each game

HOW TO PLAY: As the name implies, *Scooter Scoop Softball* combines the cognitive concepts of softball with the throwing/catching skills used in lacrosse. Set up the bases as a softball diamond, with home plate and the three bases all spaced about 30 feet apart (floor tape works best). Form two equal teams, with one team in regular softball fielding positions and the other team standing in a file formation ready to bat. The fielding players, as well as the batter, must be seated on their scooters.

The batter begins on home plate with a ball inside the scoop. He/she then throws it (as in lacrosse) out into fair territory. The rules of softball apply with base running, outs, scoring, etc., with a few exceptions— all players must move about on scooters, and fielding players can not throw the ball with their hands. Instead, a fielding player must use the scoop when "throwing" to another player. In addition, because this game is played indoors, all walls are in play.

The batting team receives one point (or "run") for each player who successfully gets back to home plate.

VARIATION: Instead of three outs, consider having the teams switch after each member of the batting team has had a chance at batting.

Scooter Hockey Softball

SKILLS/OBJECTIVES: Floor hockey striking, softball knowledge, team work

NUMBER OF PLAYERS: Arrange the players into two equal teams

EQUIPMENT: One scooter and short hockey stick for each player; one plastic hockey puck, floor tape to mark the four bases for each game

HOW TO PLAY: As the name implies, *Scooter Hockey Softball* combines the cognitive concepts of softball with the striking skills used in Scooter Hockey. Set up the bases as a softball diamond, with home plate and the three bases all spaced about 30 feet apart. Form two equal teams, with one team in regular softball fielding positions and the other team standing in a file formation ready to bat. The fielding players, as well as the batter, must be seated on their scooters.

The batter begins the game by placing the puck down on home plate, and striking it (as in floor hockey) out into fair territory. The rules of softball apply with base running, outs, scoring, etc., with a few exceptions—all players must move about on scooters, and fielding players can not throw the puck. Instead, a fielding player must strike the puck when "throwing" to another player. In addition, because this game is played indoors, all walls are in play.

The batting team receives one point (or "run") for each player who successfully gets back to home plate.

VARIATION: Instead of three outs, consider having the teams switch after each member of the batting team has had a chance at batting.

Around The Horn

SKILLS/OBJECTIVES: Throwing, catching, scooter movement, team work

NUMBER OF PLAYERS: Arrange the players into two teams of 8 players each

EQUIPMENT: One scooter for each player; one whiffle ball, floor tape to mark the four bases for each game

HOW TO PLAY: *Around the Horn* is a fun, relay-type game that utilizes the softball skills of throwing, catching, and base running (on scooters). Set up the bases as a softball diamond, with home plate and the three bases all spaced about 30 feet apart (floor tape works best). Form two teams of eight players each. The fielding team positions two players each at the four bases. The other team stands in a file formation ready to "bat" (that is, ready to run). All players must be seated on their scooters.

On a starting signal, the catcher throws the ball to first base and on around the other bases while, at the same time, the runner attempts to scoot around and touch each base. The fielders must throw the ball "around the horn" twice while the base runner only has to circle the bases once. Fielders must touch their base before throwing to the next baseman. In addition, one of two fielders at each base takes the first throw and the second player takes the second throw.

A team receives one point (or "run") for each base runner who successfully scoots back to home plate before the ball arrives.

48

Scooter Volleyball

SKILLS/OBJECTIVES: Volleyball skills (serving, setting, striking, bumping), catching, throwing, team work

NUMBER OF PLAYERS: Arrange the players into two equal teams of 3-6 players each; for large groups, set up additional play areas and play multiple games simultaneously

EQUIPMENT: One scooter for each player; a volleyball (or beach ball), a volleyball net (or substitute a tennis net)

HOW TO PLAY: Divide the players into two teams, with an equal number of players on each (3-6 players is ideal). Set up a low net (about 5' high) across the play area, and assign each team to one side of the net. Have each team line up in regular volleyball positions with each player seated on a scooter.

Scooter Volleyball is played mainly with regular volleyball rules. However, the player options of catching the volleyball and throwing it on a serve are included. One team starts the game with a serve, which can be thrown or hit over the net. The serve must travel completely over the net and land in the opponent's court—and, the server has only one chance to do so. The receiving team attempts to return the served ball with an overhead pass or bump. Any ball caught has to be self-set and immediately hit over the net or to teammates. A loss of serve or point occurs when a player hits the ball twice in a row (without being touched by another player in-between hits) or out of bounds, fails to return the ball on the team's third hit, or falls off the scooter while in possession of the ball. The team which regains the opportunity to serve must rotate its players one position clockwise. The first team to reach 15 points wins the game.

Scooter Scoopball

SKILLS/OBJECTIVES: Lacrosse-type skills (throwing and catching with plastic scoops and balls), team work

NUMBER OF PLAYERS: Arrange the players into two equal teams

EQUIPMENT: One scooter and plastic scoop for each player; one whiffle ball, colored jerseys for each team, two basketball backboards

HOW TO PLAY: *Scooter Scoopball* is played on a regular basketball court with two backboards. The objective is to hit the opponent's backboard with the whiffle ball (using a plastic scoop) while moving on a scooter.

Form two equal teams (6-8 players is ideal). Each team is assigned a specific backboard to defend. Before starting, players can position themselves at any spot around the court, but all must be seated on scooters and have their own plastic scoop.

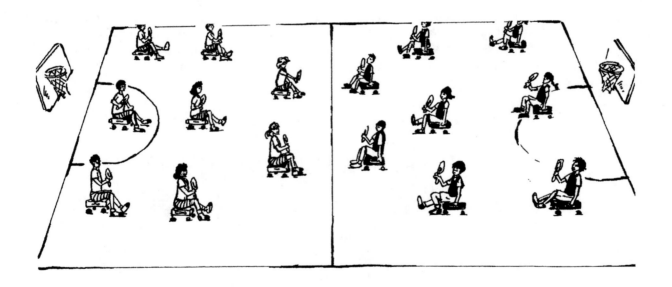

The game leader begins by giving the game ball to a designated player at mid-court to start play. This player, using his/her scoop, throws the ball to a teammate. The offensive team tries to move the ball toward the opponent's backboard by throwing and catching with the scoops, and attempts to score by throwing and hitting their backboard (worth one point). The offensive player in possession the ball is allowed to move on his/her scooter, but has only 5 seconds to pass or shoot for a score. All other offensive players are free to move anywhere on the court. Any player with possession of the ball who exceeds the 5 second rule must forfeit the ball to the other team at that spot.

Scooter Scoopball (continued)

At the same time, the defensive players (the team without the ball) attempt to intercept a pass or scoop up a loose ball. However, at no time can a defensive player touch or make any contact with an offensive player. Since this game is played indoors, the ball can be played off the walls. No player is allowed to leave his or her scooter at any time during play.

After each score, the non-scoring team starts play by passing the ball in from behind the backboard (as in basketball).

Fun & Active Games

Scooter Exercise Circuit

SKILLS/OBJECTIVES: Scooter movement skills, cardiovascular fitness

NUMBER OF PLAYERS: Unlimited; students are arranged in groups of four

EQUIPMENT: Two scooters, four traffic cones, and a large exercise task chart

HOW TO PLAY: This fun and fast-paced activity can be used as part of a fitness lesson, as a relay game, or as a warm-up activity in physical education.

Tape a large exercise/scooter movement chart on the wall visible so all can read. For each team, set four cones (approximately 15-20 feet apart) in a straight line leading outward from an end line. Group the class into teams of four; have each team stand in a file formation on the end line next to their assigned cones. Two scooters are placed in front of each team.

On a starting signal, the player at the front of each line takes a scooter and performs the specific scooter traveling movement listed on the chart on their way to the first cone. Once there, they perform the specific exercise as listed on the chart, and do the listed scooter movement to the next cone. When the first player reaches the third cone, the next teammate in line takes a scooter and starts the exercise circuit. After completing all four exercises, they scoot back to their team, go to the back of the line, and wait for their next turn. Play continues in this fashion for specified time.

Scooter Exercise Circuit (continued)

Some sample exercises the students can do at each cone include push-ups, jumping jacks, curl-ups, mountain climbers, and standing stretches. Some listed scooter movements can include lying on the stomach and using just hands to cone #1, kneeling and using hands to cone #2, sitting and using legs to cone #3, and one knee on the scooter using one leg to cone #4.

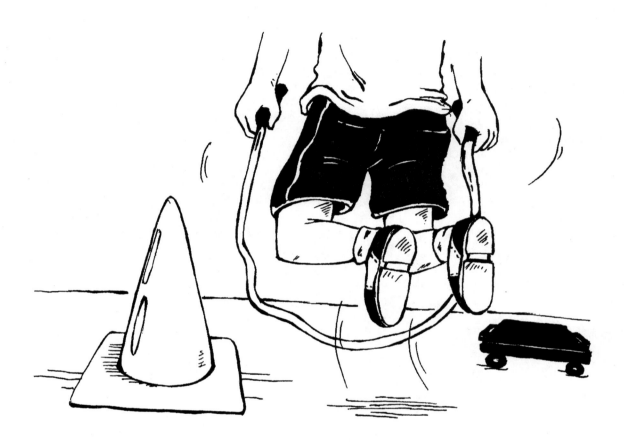

Scooter Aerobic Partners

SKILLS/OBJECTIVES: Scooter skills, cardiovascular fitness

NUMBER OF PLAYERS: Unlimited; students are arranged in pairs

EQUIPMENT: One scooter for each pair of students

HOW TO PLAY: This is a great activity to use as part of a fitness lesson, or as a warm-up activity in physical education.

Place four cones on each corner of the gymnasium. Have students choose a partner and stand facing each other along a sideline. The partner on the outside of the circle has a scooter stationed by his or her feet. A chart of various exercises should be visible for everyone to read.

On a starting signal, the partner on the outside of the line sits on the scooter and moves as quickly as possible around the four cones (1 lap). At the same time, their partner begins to perform a designated exercise as shown on a large chart. When the first scooting partner completes his or her lap, the partners change places and repeat the tasks. They continue this routine until each is finished with the alternating scooting/exercise list.

Some sample exercises the students can do include:

- Push-ups
- Jumping Jacks
- Curl-ups
- Mountain Climbers
- Sitting Stretches
- Standing Stretches

Scooter Noodle Fencing

SKILLS/OBJECTIVES: Coordination, agility

NUMBER OF PLAYERS: Unlimited; arrange the players into pairs

EQUIPMENT: One scooter and one pool noodle for each player

HOW TO PLAY: This fun one-on-one game, a modification of Fencing, utilizes pool noodles available in most physical education catalogs.

Arrange the players into pairs. Each student starts with a scooter and pool noodle.

Using the pool noodle, the objective is to make contact with one of the opponent's feet for a score (worth one point), while at the same time, avoid having the feet hit by the opponent. Players can move around, pick up their feet, and use their noodles to avoid contact. Play continues in this fashion for a predetermined number of points.

The following rules must be observed during play:

- Players cannot swing their noodles above waist level (remember, they're sitting on scooters)
- Players have to seated on their bottoms with the feet used for movement
- At no time are players allowed to leave their scooter

VARIATION: Instead of one-on-one, use *Scooter Noodle Fencing* as a whole group activity where it's "everyone against everyone." This makes for a great class energizer!

Scooter Swimmers

SKILLS/OBJECTIVES: Beginning arm movements associated with swimming, upper body strength development, agility, coordination

NUMBER OF PLAYERS: Unlimited

EQUIPMENT: One scooter for each player

HOW TO PLAY: Swimming without a pool? You bet, with a little imagination, we can turn the scooter into a "swimming board." This activity is terrific for developing upper body strength, as well as introducing various swim strokes to your students. The following description is set up as a relay (a "swim meet"), but it can also be used as part of a station lesson or simply as a challenge activity.

First, introduce the "breast stroke" and "crawl stroke" to the students and allow plenty of free practice time. Next, have the student pair up and practice the "backstroke," with two scooters under the swimmer (who is lying on his or her back) and one partner helping and guiding. Finally, introduce the "turtle turn" on a wall (the technique used by swimmers in which they turn and push off the pool wall with their feet).

After the students have mastered the above skills, consider having a "Swim Meet." Basically, it would be played as a regular relay with teams of 2-4 players, swim lanes using floor tape or traffic cones, and a wall for executing the turtle turns.

Have fun swimming!

Scooter Boxing

SKILLS/OBJECTIVES: Coordination, agility

NUMBER OF PLAYERS: Unlimited; arrange the players into pairs

EQUIPMENT: One scooter for each player

HOW TO PLAY: This fun one-on-one game utilizes the concepts of boxing—but without the pain!

Arrange the players into pairs. Each student starts in a seated position on a scooter with the feet used for traveling.

Without kicking or stomping, the objective is to use your feet to make contact with an opponent's foot for a score (worth one point), while at the same time, avoid having your feet touched by the opponent. Players can move around and pick up their feet to avoid contact. Play continues in this fashion for a predetermined number of points.

The following rules must be observed during play:
- Players cannot kick or stomp
- Players have to seated on their bottoms with the feet used for movement
- At no time are players allowed to leave their scooter

VARIATION: Instead of one-on-one, use *Scooter Foot Boxing* as a whole group activity where it's "everyone against everyone." This makes for a great class energizer!

States & Capitols

SKILLS/OBJECTIVES: Scooter skills, fitness

NUMBER OF PLAYERS: Unlimited

EQUIPMENT: One scooter for each player

HOW TO PLAY: *States & Capitols* is a scooter version of the popular game Crows & Cranes. However, this activity provides an opportunity to link geography and physical education.

Divide the players into two equal teams. Designate one team as the "States" and the other as "Capitols." The groups face each other in the center of the playing area, about 5 feet apart, with all sitting on scooters. The two basketball court sidelines create safety lines behind each group.

The leader calls out either the name of a state, such as Oregon, or the name of a capitol, such as Salem. The team being called chases the other team while on the scooters. The team being chased must quickly turn and scoot for safety behind their safety line. Once behind the safety line, players cannot be tagged. The chasers tag as many players as they can; with the tagged players becoming members of the chasing team for the next round of play. The winning team is the one with the most players at the conclusion of play.

Players must remain seated or kneeling on their scooters at all times.

VARIATION: Consider playing *Scooter Crows & Cranes* for the younger students or those who have yet to study United States geography. The setup and rules are same as described above, but now the leader simply calls out "Crows" or "Cranes."

Scooter Bear

SKILLS/OBJECTIVES: Scooter skills, cardiovascular fitness

NUMBER OF PLAYERS: Unlimited

EQUIPMENT: One scooter for each player

HOW TO PLAY: *Scooter Bear* is a modified version of the popular game of Little Brown Bear. It's also a great activity for practicing and reviewing the various ways of moving on a scooter.

This game is best played using the two sidelines of a half basketball court. Select one player to start in the middle as the "Bear." The other players position themselves along one sideline. All players are seated on scooters.

The game begins with the Bear calling out, "Who's afraid of the Bear?" The other players reply with "Not me." The Bear then replies, "Then I want you scoot through the woods to the other side by seating on your bottom." All of the players must move exactly as stated through the woods to the other sideline. Using the same movement, the Bear tries to tag as many players as possible. Players who are tagged become Bear's "helpers," and join the Bear in the middle for the next call. The game continues with the Bear calling out a different method of scooting each time. The game ends when all of the players have been caught.

Before play, it might be helpful to review all the different methods of moving on a scooter (kneeling, sitting, etc.)

Roll The Dice

SKILLS/OBJECTIVES: Reinforcement of math concepts, scooter skills, cardiovascular fitness

NUMBER OF PLAYERS: Unlimited; arrange students into pairs

EQUIPMENT: One scooter for each player; one pair of dice for each pair of students

HOW TO PLAY: *Roll the Dice* as described below is a one-on-one activity; however, it can be played with larger groups by using the jumbo-sized foam dice available in many physical education catalogs. This is a great game for mixing movement with the reinforcement of math concepts.

This game is best played using the two sidelines of a basketball court as the safety lines. Position two players on scooters about 3-4 feet apart in the middle between the two sidelines. Designate one player as the "Odd" player, and the other as "Even." One player starts with the dice in hand.

Before rolling the dice, the class instructor announces the mathematical function the players are to perform. For example, "Add the two numbers together that appear on the dice when they come to a stop." After one of the players rolls the dice, they add the two numbers. If it's an even number, the "Even" player chases the "Odd" player back to his or her safety line. If the answer is an odd number, the "Odd" player chases the "Even" player. One point is awarded to the chaser who successfully tags the other player before reaching the safety line. After each turn, the players return to the middle and play again.

Other mathematical challenges can be subtracting the smaller-numbered dice from the higher-numbered dice, and multiplying the two numbers displayed.

Egg Hunt

SKILLS/OBJECTIVES: Scooter skills, cardiovascular fitness

NUMBER OF PLAYERS: Unlimited; students are arranged in teams of four

EQUIPMENT: One scooter for each team; 25 traffic cones, 25 beanbags (an equal number of five different colors

HOW TO PLAY: This activity simulates the excitement of an Easter egg hunt.

Scatter 25 beanbags (an equal number of 5 different colors) on half of a basketball court; place a traffic cone over the top of each beanbag so all are hidden. Divide the class into teams of four. Each team lines up behind the end line in a file formation. A scooter is placed at the front of each line. Assign each team a specific colored beanbag they are to retrieve.

The objective is to be the first group to retrieve their five colored beanbags (or Easter eggs). On a starting signal, the first person from each group moves on their scooter out to a cone, picks it up, takes the beanbag lying underneath if it's the correct color, and scoots back to starting line placing the beanbag in front of the team. If a player picks up a cone and the beanbag is not the color they need, the cone must be immediately placed back over the top of the beanbag, and the player returns empty-handed. In turn, the players scoot out and look for the correct-colored beanbags until all five have been retrieved.

Only one cone can be picked per turn. Also, players are not allowed to look through the top of the cone before picking it up.

Scooter Blitz

SKILLS/OBJECTIVES: Cardiovascular fitness, scooter skills

NUMBER OF PLAYERS: Unlimited; arrange the players into two equal teams.

EQUIPMENT: One scooter for each player; 20-50 lightweight plastic bowling pins

HOW TO PLAY: This high-energy game is a fun warm-up activity.

In a gymnasium, place the plastic bowling pins randomly throughout the playing area, with all of them standing. Divide the class into two equal teams. Each team lines up along a designated sideline, with each player sitting on a scooter. To begin, one team will start out as the "knocker-downers," and the other team as the "set'em uppers."

On a starting signal, the "knocker-downer" team quickly scoots around and attempts to knock over the bowling pins (using their hands) with the objective of knocking over as many as possible. Meanwhile, the "set'em upper" team scoots out into the play area and quickly sets up as many downed pins. At the end of one minute, the group that has more pins in their desired position (standing or knocked over) is the winner. Have the teams change roles and repeat the game.

Caution the "set'em uppers" to not interfere or block any of the "knocker-downers" from knocking over the pins.

Scooter Doctors

SKILLS/OBJECTIVES: Rolling, scooter movement, team work

NUMBER OF PLAYERS: Unlimited; arrange the players into two equal teams

EQUIPMENT: One scooter for each player; 12-24 large-size foam ball, 4 colored jerseys for each team's doctors

HOW TO PLAY: This exciting game is played on a regular basketball court with two equal-size teams facing each other from opposite sides of the center line. The center line divides the two teams. Each team has two players, wearing colored jerseys, who are designated as the "doctors." Hand out an equal number of balls (12 or more) to players on each team. All players must be seated on scooters.

On a starting signal, the players may move about anywhere on their side of the play area and try to roll a ball at a player on the other team. If hit, that player must sit on the floor with his or her scooter turned upside down. The team doctors may rescue those hit by touching the injured teammate on the shoulder. Once rescued, players may sit on their scooter and resume play once again. A doctor can also be hit at any time and can only be rescued by the remaining doctor. When both doctors have been eliminated on a side, the game ends with the opposing team victorious.

Players are not allowed to throw or kick the balls (only rolling). In addition, players are required to seated on their scooter at all times during play.

Scooter Square Dancing

SKILLS/OBJECTIVES: Listening skills, cooperation

NUMBER OF PLAYERS: Unlimited; form groups of eight students

EQUIPMENT: One scooter for each player; square dance music

HOW TO PLAY: Here is a favorite with the younger students—square dancing on scooters without holding hands. For those who have taught dance to elementary-age students, you know how "painful" the hand-holding requirement can be for some students. For those who want, a holding-hands dance variation is included on the next page. Both are great activities for incorporating listening skills.

Have the students pair up. Depending on the number of students, set up several dance square formations with 8 participants each. In each group, choose two couples to be the "head" couples; and two couples to perform as the "Side" couples (see illustration). All are seated on scooters, and face the couple on the opposite side of the square.

Most likely, the square dancing music with the calls included is going to be a little too fast for students moving on scooters. As a consequence, it's recommended that you use call-less square dance music in the background with the leader calling and directing the groups in a variety of square dance movements. Square dance and western-style music CD's are available in most physical education catalogs.

Scooter Square Dancing (continued)

Some ideas for calls are:

- "Into the center and back" – Both partners stay close together and move to the center of the square and back.
- "Circle your partner right," Circle to the left" – Without holding hands, the partners circle each other.
- "Dos-sa-do your partner" – Same as above with arms crossed
- "Bow to your Corner ," Bow to your Partner" – While seated on a scooter, bow head toward the person on the opposite side of partner.
- "Stomp your feet , clap, and shout!"
- "All promenade around the circle" – Without hands, move side-by-side with partner clockwise around the square.
- "Head couples Dos-sa-do," Side Couples Dos-a-do"

VARIATION: Consider regular square dancing on scooters—but, with hands (see illustration below). The organization and setup is the same as above, but now the calls can include movements that require hand holding, clapping partner's hands, swinging partners with the arms, allemande with the hands, and so forth.

Scooter Limbo

SKILLS/OBJECTIVES: Scooter skills, agility

NUMBER OF PLAYERS: Unlimited

EQUIPMENT: One scooter for each player; one pool noodle or yardstick for each group, music

HOW TO PLAY: This popular activity is a scooter version of regular Limbo. Although optional, *Scooter Limbo* is more fun when upbeat music is played, such as Chubby Checker's hit tune from the 1960's called "Limbo Rock." Depending on the number of students, set up several limbo lines with 4-5 participants each. Choose two students in each group to hold the limbo stick about head high at first—remember, the students are seated on scooters. The safest limbo stick would be a pool noodle (available in most physical education catalogs). The other students form a line.

    In turn, the students move on their scooters underneath (facing upward) the stick without touching it, or falling backwards off the scooter. After each round, select new holders and adjust the limbo stick lower and lower. Repeat this process until only one player is left.

Gym Closet Race

SKILLS/OBJECTIVES: Scooter skills, cardiovascular fitness

NUMBER OF PLAYERS: Unlimited; students are arranged in teams of three players

EQUIPMENT: Six scooters and hoops; seven each of six objects depicting a wide variety of physical education equipment (beanbags, whistles, hockey pucks, whiffle balls, fleece balls, tennis balls, track batons, kicking tees, and so forth).

HOW TO PLAY: Using the basketball court, place a hoop in each corner and two on opposite sidelines by the half-court line. In each hoop place all six of one item, such as the beanbags. The seventh piece (in this case the last beanbag) is placed outside the hoop to later remind players what piece of equipment is to go inside the hoop. A scooter is set beside each hoop. Assign three players to a hoop (this number can be increased if there are extra players).

On a starting signal, the first player from each team sits on the scooter, takes one item out of his or her team's hoop, and proceeds to scoot to the other hoops taking one item at a time. When this player returns (with all six items), he or she immediately hands the items and scooter to the next player in line. This player returns the items, one at a time, with the last item being the one from their own hoop. Continue this alternating routine until everyone has had two turns. The team finishing first wins the contest.

During play, the items must be carried; they may not be thrown, kicked, or pushed along the floor.

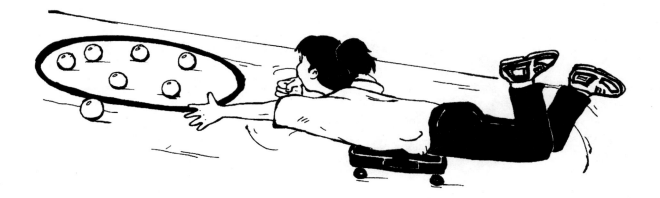

Scooter Express

SKILLS/OBJECTIVES: Scooter skills, cardiovascular fitness, team work

NUMBER OF PLAYERS: Unlimited; form teams of four players each

EQUIPMENT: One scooter and one beanbag for each group of four players; four cones

HOW TO PLAY: Using a large open area in the gymnasium, design an oval shape course similar to the one shown in the diagram. Place a cone at four stations on the course. Divide the players into teams of four players each, and assign players from each team to start at one of the four stations. The players at station #1 start with a beanbag and a scooter.

On a starting signal, the players at station #1 begin scooting and carry their beanbags to the teammates at station #2. After handing off the beanbag and scooter (no throwing allowed), the players from station #1 stay at station #2. The players from station #2 carry the beanbag to their teammates at station #3, hand off the beanbag and scooter, and stay there. The players from station #3 carries the beanbags to station #4, switch scooters, and stay there. The players from station #4 have to carry the beanbag all the way (two segments) to the next teammates who are now at station #2. Every player at station #4 will have to scoot double duty throughout the game. Play continues in this fashion until all of the players are back in their original starting positions. The objective is to be the first team to finish the race.

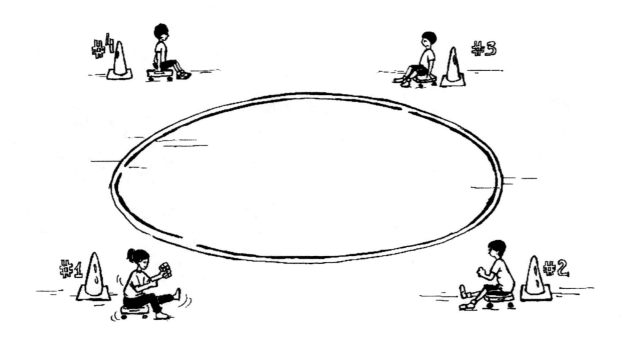

70

Canoe Rafting

SKILLS/OBJECTIVES: Scooter skills, cardiovascular fitness, arm-shoulder strength

NUMBER OF PLAYERS: Unlimited; form teams of three players each

EQUIPMENT: One scooter and cone for each team

HOW TO PLAY: This fun relay imitates the arm movement used in canoeing.

Form groups of three players each. Each group lines in a single file on a starting line (the basketball court sidelines work great as starting and turnaround spots). The first player on each team begins with a scooter and one small-size cone.

On a starting signal, the first player on each team, kneeling on his or her scooter and using the cone, attempts to "canoe" to the turning point and back. The alternating arm movements are made with the cone being held upside down, and at no time are players allowed to use their hands. The next player may leave when handed the scooter and "canoe paddle."

The relay ends when all of the canoes have arrived back to the starting line.

Wide World of Sports

SKILLS/OBJECTIVES: Scooter skills, cardiovascular fitness

NUMBER OF PLAYERS: Unlimited; students are arranged in pairs

EQUIPMENT: One scooter and hoop for each pair of students; traffic cones, boxes containing a wide variety of sport balls and equipment

HOW TO PLAY: This invigorating activity can be used as part of a fitness lesson or warm-up activity in physical education.

   With the cones, make a track around the gymnasium. Around the inside of the track, place enough evenly-spaced hula hoops for each pair of students. In the middle of the play area, place boxes containing a variety of sport balls and equipment—the more the better! Two students are assigned to each hoop which contains a scooter.

   The objective is to be the first group to have five separate pieces of sport equipment. On a starting signal, one person from each group scoots one time around the track back to his or her hoop, sets the scooter upside down beside the hoop, and runs over to the box of sport balls. This student then picks one item and places it in the hoop. When finished, the next partner takes the scooter, completes one lap around the track, and completes the same task. This switching continues throughout the game. Some sample sport equipment the students can grab can include items such as basketballs, footballs, softballs, volleyballs, soccer balls, hockey pucks, kicking tees, hockey sticks, softball bats, and so forth.

72

Speedboats

SKILLS/OBJECTIVES: Scooter skills, cardiovascular fitness

NUMBER OF PLAYERS: Unlimited; group the players into teams of three

EQUIPMENT: Two scooters, one folded gym mat for each team; 6-12 cone markers

HOW TO PLAY: With the cone markers, set up an oval shaped water "track" around the gym. Arrange the players into teams of three players. Each team begins with a folded tumbling mat resting on two scooters on the starting line. One player is the "driver" and sits (or lies down) on the mat with the other teammates (the "engine") stationed behind the "speedboat."

On a starting signal, the engines (the two teammates behind the boat with their hands on the mat) push and guide their boats once around the lake back to the starting line. Once there, the players switch places so a new driver is now in the boat (that is, sitting on top of the mat). The new engine pushes the boat back once around the lake, they switch places, etc. The race continues until everyone has had a turn at being the speedboat driver. The first speedboat over the finish line wins.

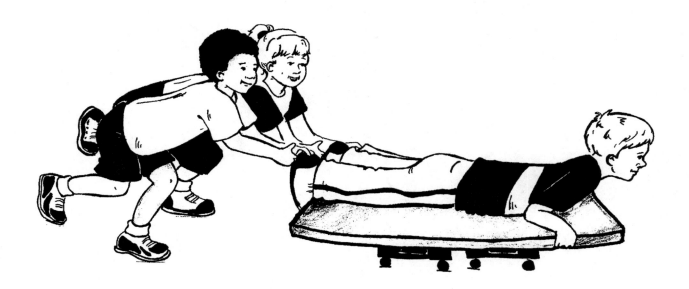

Capture The Beanbags

SKILLS/OBJECTIVES: Scooter movements, team work

NUMBER OF PLAYERS: Unlimited; arrange the players into two equal teams

EQUIPMENT: One scooter and team identification jersey for each player; six beanbags, cone markers, floor tape

HOW TO PLAY: *Capture the Beanbags* is a variation of the traditional game Capture the Flag.

Divide the players into two teams and assign each team to one-half of the playing area (a basketball court with lines works best). Have players of each team wear identification jerseys of the same color and seated on a scooter.

Using floor tape, set up the play area as shown in the diagram. Place three beanbags in each team's bank. Each team is allowed to have a guard located by the jail, and another guard by the bank. The remaining players scatter on their half of the play area.

On a signal, players can cross the center line and try to steal the beanbags from the other team's bank. However, players are allowed to only grab one beanbag at a time. In addition, when they cross over into the other team's territory, they can tagged (a touch on the identification jersey) and jailed by an opponent. If tagged they go to that team's jail.

Capture the Beanbags (continued)

    A player can escape from jail if a teammate can successfully scoot into the jail, grab his or her inside hand, and maintain joined hands until back across the center line. Opponents cannot tag players who are making their way back from being rescued from jail as long as the inside hands are joined. The jail guard is never allowed to go into the jail.

    If a player who has picked up a beanbag and is trying to reach safety is caught, the beanbag is returned to the bank and that player goes to jail. At no time can a player throw or kick a beanbag.

    The game continues until one side has all six beanbags (their three plus the opponent's three beanbags), or until all the players from one side are jailed.

Scooter Squirrels

SKILLS/OBJECTIVES: Scooter movement, cardiovascular fitness

NUMBER OF PLAYERS: 8-12 players to a game; set up multiple play areas for large groups

EQUIPMENT: One scooter for each of the 4 teams; 6 beanbags for each game; floor tape or five hula hoops

HOW TO PLAY: With the floor tape, design five circles (2-3 feet in diameter) or substitute hula hoops. Place 6 beanbags (or "acorns") in the middle circle. Divide players into four teams and have each team form a line behind their own circle (or "home"). The first player in line begins with the scooter.

The objective is to the first team with three acorns in their home circle. On a starting signal, the first player on each team scoots to the middle circle, takes one beanbag, goes back to his or her home, and places the beanbag in the circle. This player immediately gives the scooter to the next teammate and goes to the back of the line. In turn, players keep taking beanbags from the middle circle until it is empty, at which point players can steal beanbags from each other's circles. Since teams cannot defend the beanbags in its home circle, there is always a place from which to steal a beanbag. The first team to store up three "acorns" is the winner. A player may only take one beanbag per turn.

If the game is too easy, increase the number of beanbags in the middle circle and the number needed to win.

Give Away

SKILLS/OBJECTIVES: Scooter movement, cardiovascular fitness

NUMBER OF PLAYERS: 4 players to a game; set up multiple play areas for large groups

EQUIPMENT: One scooter for each of the 4 players; 8 beanbags for each game; floor tape or 4 hula hoops

HOW TO PLAY: With the floor tape, design four circles (2-3 feet in diameter) or substitute hula hoops. Place two beanbags in each circle. One player sits on a scooter by each of the four circles. For large-size groups, set up multiple play areas and play several games simultaneously.

Each player's objective is to get rid of his or her two beanbags first, one at a time, by depositing them into other players' circles. On a starting signal, each player grabs one beanbag, scoots to an opponent's circle and places it inside their circle. They immediately scoot back to their own circle and repeat the same process again. Play continues until one player has no beanbags left in his or her circle.

If the game is too easy, consider adding additional beanbags.

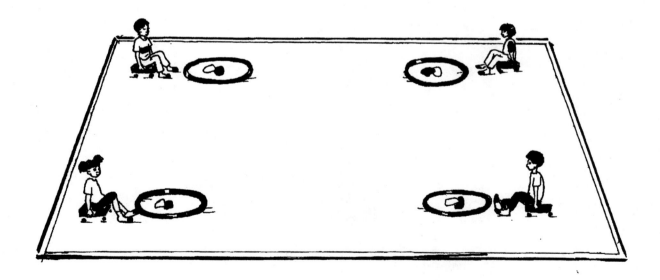

Mountain Rescue

SKILLS/OBJECTIVES: Upper body strength development, team work

NUMBER OF PLAYERS: Unlimited; students are arranged in equal-sized groups of threes

EQUIPMENT: Each group will need one scooter and a clothesline rope of 30 feet or longer

HOW TO PLAY: This activity can be played as a relay, part of a "station" lesson, or simply as a fun challenge. For older students, consider playing with one of the variations described below.

Divide the students into groups of threes. For each team, lay one clothesline rope lengthwise across the basketball court. Position two teammates at one end of the rope; the third teammate lies on his or her stomach on a scooter and holds on the other end of the rope. When ready, one partner at the rope end begins pulling hand over hand, while the other rope partner takes the slack and circles it on the floor. The person on the scooter being rescued cannot use legs, arms, or assist in any way. When successfully pulled over to the two partners, the rescued player switches with one of the rope partners, and now this player has a chance to get "rescued." Play continues in this fashion until all three players have had chances to be rescued.

VARIATION: This activity can be made more challenging by using one puller, one person lying on a carpet square, and one person lying on a scooter who has his or her ankles held by the carpet square player. Another alternative is to have two players lying on scooters (one player holding the ankles of the other) and both being pulled by one player.

Scooter Pin Ball

SKILLS/OBJECTIVES: Rolling, scooter movement, team work

NUMBER OF PLAYERS: Unlimited; arrange the players into two equal teams

EQUIPMENT: One scooter and playground ball for each player; 12 plastic bowling pins, floor tape

HOW TO PLAY: *Scooter Pin Ball* is played on a regular basketball court with two equal-size teams facing each other from opposite sides of the center line. The center line divides the two teams. Six bowling pins, evenly spaced, are placed on each end line. With the floor tape, mark off a restraining line about 10 feet in front of the pins. Hand out an equal number of balls to players on each team (one for each player is ideal). All players must be seated on scooters.

The object of the game is to roll balls at the opponent's pins, attempting to knock over all six. On a starting signal, the players may move about anywhere on their side of the center line and attempt to roll a ball at the opponent's pins. Once knocked over, a pin is down and cannot be set back up. Players are not allowed to defend their pins inside the restraining area—in fact, players can cross their restraining line only to retrieve loose balls. However, rolled balls can be knocked away or intercepted between the restraining and center lines.

A winner is declared once all pins on one side are knocked over. If this doesn't occur, whoever has the most pins standing at the end of play is declared the winner.

Players are not to throw or kick the balls; only rolling is allowed. In addition, players have to be seated on their scooters at all times.

Deep Sea Diving

SKILLS/OBJECTIVES: Upper body strength development, cardiovascular fitness

NUMBER OF PLAYERS: Unlimited; students are arranged in teams of three or more players

EQUIPMENT: One scooter , one hoop, one tumbling mat, ten traffic cones, three yardsticks, and six each of a specific colored beanbag for each team

HOW TO PLAY: Using the basketball court, place a hoop in each corner (for larger groups, place two hoops on opposite sidelines by the half-court line). A scooter is set beside each hoop. Leading outward from the hoop to the center circle, place a row of three cones with yardsticks resting on top, and a folded tumbling mat resting on cones. Assign 3-4 players to a hoop (this number can be increased if there are extra players). In the basketball mid-court circle, place six of same colored beanbags for each team. Assign each team a specific colored beanbag to retrieve.

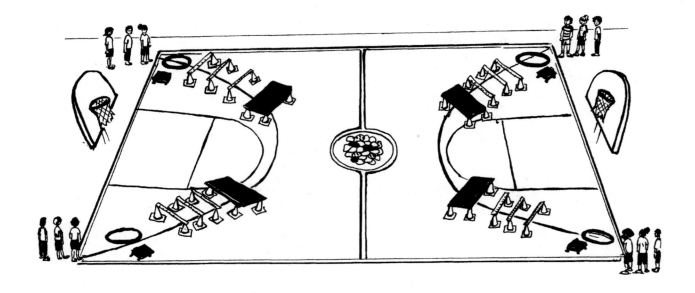

The objective is to be the first group to successfully travel ("deep sea diving") under the obstacles and retrieve their six pieces of treasure (the colored beanbags). On a starting signal, the first player from each team travels on the scooter under the three hockey sticks and tumbling mat, retrieves one of their assigned colored beanbags, travels back through the obstacles and places the beanbag in the team's hoop. At that

Deep Sea Diving (continued)

time, the next teammate in line goes "deep sea diving." Play continues in this fashion until each team has retrieved its six beanbags.

Team members may not touch the cones, yardsticks, or mats. If they do, they must return back to their team without the treasure (beanbag). In addition, the treasure must be carried; it cannot be thrown, kicked, or pushed along the floor.

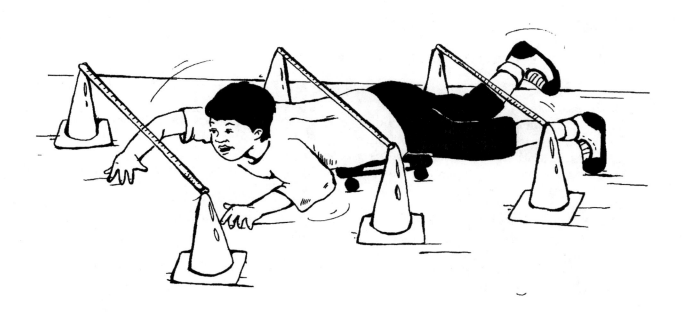

Mountain Rope Traversing

SKILLS/OBJECTIVES: Upper body strength development, team work

NUMBER OF PLAYERS: Unlimited; students are arranged in groups of threes

EQUIPMENT: Each team will need 1 clothesline rope (50 feet or longer) and one scooter

HOW TO PLAY: As with *Mountain Rescue* (see page 78), this activity can be played as a relay, part of a station lesson, or simply as a fun challenge.

Divide the students into groups of threes. For each group, lay one clothesline rope lengthwise across the gym. Two teammates, one at each end of the rope, pull the rope so there is no slack. The third teammate, lying on a scooter that is positioned over the rope at one end, begins pulling hand over hand to the other side. Once there, he or she changes places with the rope holder who now crosses the gym. Play continues in this fashion until everyone has had a chance at traversing across the gym.

VARIATIONS: For added challenge, have the students perform the following activities:
- Have the traversing student lie on his or back while pulling. The rope holders will have to hold the rope over the scooter rather than underneath it.
- Increase the length of the traverse by having the students pull across the gym and back; or increase the length of the rope.

Daytona Speedway

SKILLS/OBJECTIVES: Scooter skills, cardiovascular fitness

NUMBER OF PLAYERS: Unlimited; form teams of two or three players each

EQUIPMENT: Two scooters for each team; 6-12 cone markers

HOW TO PLAY: With the cone markers, set up an oval shaped track around the gym. Inside the track, close to the starting line, set up an area to be known as the "pit stop" area. Arrange the players into teams of two or three players. Each team begins with a player (the "driver") resting on two scooters on the starting line (their bottom on one scooter and feet on the other). The other teammates (the "engine") are stationed behind the "driver" with their hands placed on his or her shoulders.

On a starting signal, the engines (the one or two teammates behind the driver) push and guide their cars once around the track and into the pit stop area. Once there, the players switch places so a new driver is now in the car (that is, sitting on the two scooters). The new engine pushes the car back out into the track, go once around, back into the pit stop, switch places, etc. The race continues until everyone has had a turn at being the driver. The first car over the finish line wins.

High Sea Rescue

GRADES 3-6

SKILLS/OBJECTIVES: Scooter skills, team work

NUMBER OF PLAYERS: Unlimited; students are arranged in equal-sized teams of 4-5 players

EQUIPMENT: Each team will need 1 scooter, 2 long jump ropes, 2 poly spots, 1 tumbling mat

HOW TO PLAY: This challenging but fun activity requires lots of teamwork and group cooperation.

The play area utilizes the half-court lines on a basketball court. At one end, place a tumbling mat for each team. At the other end, place a scooter, two long jump ropes, and two poly spots for each team. Create teams of four or five players. The players begin seated in a file formation behind their equipment.

Begin by telling the students an elaborate anticipatory story about being shipwrecked on a deserted island in the middle of the sea. There are riptides, sharks, and all kinds of danger circling the islands. In the distance, there are ships (the tumbling mats) to rescue them, but because of underwater rocks, they cannot come any closer. The challenge is to get to the rescue ships without touching the water (floor).

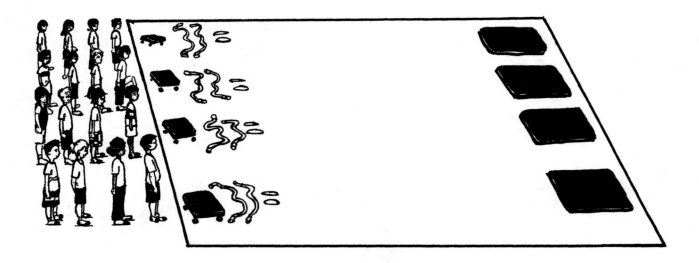

Each team has a small boat (the scooter), two poly spots, and two long ropes which can be tied together to make one extra long rope. The team members must devise a plan to get one person at a time over to the rescue ship, and return the small boat for the next team member to use. Players can not stand on their scooters or whip them across the floor; otherwise they can use the scooter, poly spots, and ropes as they wish.

High Sea Rescue (continued)

If anyone touches the water (floor) with any body part, the player along with the equipment must return to the island, and he or she goes the back of the line. Once a player successfully makes it to the rescue ship (the mat), he or she stays put. However, this person can help in handling the ropes. Play until all teams have made it safely to the rescue ships.

Some strategies for success in crossing the sea include:

- Using the poly spots to cover the hands (to avoid touching the water)
- Tying the rope(s) to the scooter handles so that the scooter can be dragged back after it has been used by a team member
- Utilizing the first team member on the rescue ship to throw ropes and pull teammates who are holding on to ropes

River Kayaking

SKILLS/OBJECTIVES: Upper body strength development, agility, coordination

NUMBER OF PLAYERS: Unlimited

EQUIPMENT: One scooter and one scooter kayak paddle for each group; traffic cones

HOW TO PLAY: *River Kayaking* imitates the arm movement used in real kayaking, creating a great opportunity to develop arm and shoulder strength. The scooter kayak paddles used in this activity can be found in most physical education catalogs. This specialized paddle is constructed from a length of plastic tubing pipe, wrapped with thin foam for good gripping, and dense rubber ends that provide good traction for paddlers.

   Divide the class into groups of 3-4 players. Assign each group to a starting line at end of the gym. The players start in a file formation behind a cone. One scooter and one kayak paddle is placed in front of each team. With traffic cones, form a winding river around the gym. The river should have a wide "mouth" at the beginning, alternating narrow and wide widths in the middle part, and a wide "outlet" at the end which leads to where the teams are located. The wide mouth allows enough space for multiple kayakers to enter at the same time. Because paddling is a fairly strenuous exercise, it would be prudent to make the river length shorter for the 3rd-5th graders and longer for the 6th-8th graders.

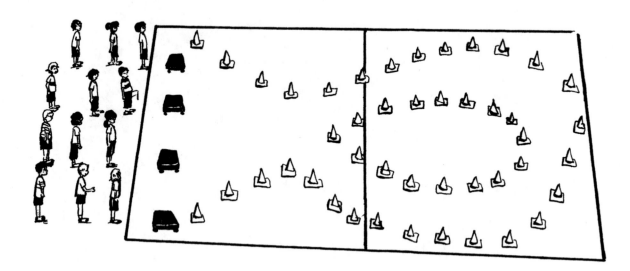

Before letting the students use the paddle, review the following tips and techniques:
- Grasp the paddle with hands wide apart, palms down, near to the ends of the paddle.
- To initiate the paddling, place one end of the paddle out in front, close to the middle, but not too close as to cause the paddle and scooter to meet.

River Kayaking (continued)

- To ensure good traction when pulling on the paddle, lean much of your body weight down on the paddle.
- Continue to keep your body weight on the paddle as you move past it, and then push hard.
- Place the other end of the paddle on the floor and repeat.

Play begins with the first player on each team "kayaking" down the river. After completing the trip, he or she hands the scooter/paddle to the next teammate in line. In turn, all the players complete their kayaking trips. Encourage the use of "helpers" when students get "grounded" (that is, unable to initiate paddling after coming to a stop).

River Kayaking can be played as a single-team challenge (for example, encourage the teams to better their "time" with each round), as a team vs. team relay, as part of a station lesson, or as an entire class movement activity if there are enough kayak paddles and scooters for all.

Scooter Skeletons

SKILLS/OBJECTIVES: Human skeletal system concepts, cardiovascular fitness, teamwork

NUMBER OF PLAYERS: Unlimited; students are arranged in teams of three or four

EQUIPMENT: One scooter, one hoop, and one skeleton puzzle for each team

HOW TO PLAY: This invigorating activity allows students an actual hands-on approach to the learning of the human skeletal system. The skeleton puzzles required for this activity can be found in many physical education catalogs and educational supply stores. If you don't have access to the puzzles, then simply put together a set of laminated skeletal pictures for each team.

Before play, review the names of major bones and, specifically, the ones that are included in the skeleton puzzle. A large chart of the entire human skeleton system should be placed on a gym wall for reference.

Divide the class into teams of three or four players. Each team lines up behind an end line in a file formation. A scooter and hoop is placed at the front of each team. Take the skeleton puzzle sets (one for each team) and scatter the bone pieces around the opposite end of the gym.

The objective is to be the first group to collect all the bones that would complete the puzzle set—and, to correctly piece together the skeleton set. On a starting signal, the first player on each team moves on their scooter to the opposite end, collects a bone, carries it back to the team's hoop and places it down. In turn, the players scoot out and retrieve the correct bones to complete the skeletal puzzle. Once they have the correct number of puzzle items, they take the bones out of the hoop and piece it together on the floor.

During play, only one bone can be retrieved per turn. Also, players have to return any extra bones not needed to complete their skeleton.

Scooter Team Handball

SKILLS/OBJECTIVES: Throwing and catching, team work

NUMBER OF PLAYERS: Arrange the players into two equal teams

EQUIPMENT: One scooter for each player; one foam ball (or similar type ball), different-colored jerseys for each team, two indoor soccer goals (or you can use tape to make goals on the two end walls that are about the size on an indoor soccer net)

HOW TO PLAY: *Scooter Team Handball* is played on a regular basketball court with two indoor soccer nets for goals. If you do not have indoor soccer nets, you can use tape to mark goals on the two end walls behind the basketball backboards. The objective is to throw the ball into the opponent's goal for a score (while moving on a scooter).

Form two equal teams (6-8 players is ideal). Each team has one player in the goalie position with the rest scattered anywhere on the court. All players must be seated on scooters.

The team designated to start on offense begins by advancing the ball down the court by throwing and catching, with the objective of throwing it into the opponent's goal for a score (worth one point). The offensive player in possession the ball can not move on the scooter, and can only pass to a teammate or shoot for a score. All other offensive players are free to move anywhere on the court. At the same time, the defensive players (the team without the ball), attempts to intercept a pass or pick up any loose ball. However, at no time can a defensive player touch or make any contact with an offensive player. No player, either offensive or defensive, is allowed to leave their scooter. Since this game is played indoors, the ball can be played off the walls.

After each score, the non-scoring team starts play by passing the ball from the mid-court area.

Team Garbage Ball

SKILLS/OBJECTIVES: Throwing and catching skills, teamwork, cardiovascular fitness

NUMBER OF PLAYERS: Unlimited; arrange the players into two equal teams

EQUIPMENT: One scooter for each player; different colored jerseys for each team; 25-40 fleece and 25-40 yarn balls

HOW TO PLAY: This fun-filled game is played somewhat like *Scooter Team Handball* (see previous game), but with many more balls and a different scoring strategy. Because of the ball-handling opportunities, it's an excellent instructional choice to improve students' throwing and catching skills.

Using the basketball court, place a box full of yarn balls at one end in the middle and a box full of fleece balls at the opposite end (an equal number of balls in each). If only one type of ball is available, consider using different colored balls for each box. In addition, next to the boxes of balls, place an empty box at each end. Divide the class into equal teams and have them go to opposites ends to sit on a scooter.

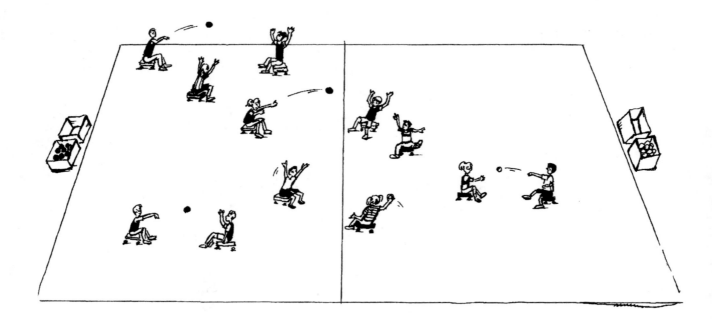

90

Team Garbage Ball (continued)

The object of the game is for each team to transfer their designated ball (yarn or fleece; or color) into their team's empty box at the opposite end of the court. On a starting signal, students may start taking balls, one at a time, out of their designated ball box (located on their end line) to throw to teammates. Once players have possession of a ball, they cannot travel forward or backward on the scooter and must immediately throw the ball. Loose balls can be picked up at any time; but again players can't travel from that spot. At no time can players play "defense", or interfere with the opponent's throwing and catching. Remind players to remain on their scooter at all times.

The first team to transfer all of their designated balls from their full box to the empty box at the opposite end is declared the winner.

Game instructors might want to emphasize the use of strategies to improve performance. That is, encourage the players to play certain position and roles, and to spread out around the court, etc.

Scootermobiles

SKILLS/OBJECTIVES: Introduction of safe "driving" on scooters and basic traffic rules; muscular strength, endurance

NUMBER OF PLAYERS: Unlimited

EQUIPMENT: One scooter for each player; a variety of props (see list below)

HOW TO PLAY: This is a great activity for reinforcing safety concepts related to riding a scooter, such as proper spacing between students, how to propel oneself safely, maintaining a safe speed, and being visually aware of the one's environment.

In the gymnasium, design a "city" landscape complete with one-way roads, tunnels, buildings, freeways, intersections, and so forth. The following props are suggested:

- Tumbling mats resting on top of traffic cones for tunnels
- Yellow floor tape to mark out railroad tracks, cross-walks, school zones, etc.
- Black floor tape to mark the roads
- Standing tumbling mats for creating alleys with tall buildings
- Cardboard boxes decorated to represent businesses, schools, etc.
- Laminated signs indicating one-way streets, construction zones, yield, etc.
- Laminated stop signs
- Jump ropes (laid in various positions) to represent obstacles to go around while traveling off-road
- Traffic cones to represent construction zones

Scootermobiles (continued)

Before play, remind students about the 'rules of the road" while operating a scooter—looking both ways at intersections, slowing down for construction zones, following arrows for one-way streets, using hand signals for turning, yielding at intersections, keeping safe distances between vehicles, and so forth. The game instructor is the police officer watching for traffic violations.

Place the students at various locations around the "city" and let them begin!

Food Pyramid Race

SKILLS/OBJECTIVES: Reinforcement of nutrition and food concepts, scooter skills, cardiovascular fitness

NUMBER OF PLAYERS: Unlimited; students are arranged in groups of three or four

EQUIPMENT: One scooter and laminated food pyramid poster for each team; laminated pictures depicting a wide variety of foods

HOW TO PLAY: This scooter activity allows students to review the food pyramid, healthy eating concepts—and, have fun at the same time! Food Pyramid posters and charts can be found in many of the physical education catalogs, as well as in educational supply stores.

Before play, review with the class the food pyramid, types of foods that represent each category, the number of food servings people should eat each day, healthy eating habits, etc.

Scatter the laminated food pictures on half of a basketball court. Divide the class into teams of three or four. Each team lines up behind the opposite end line in a file formation. A scooter is placed at the front of each line, and a laminated food pyramid chart placed behind each team.

The objective is to be the first group to complete the food pyramid. On a starting signal, the first person from each group moves on their scooter out to a food picture, picks it up, takes it back to his or her team's food chart, and places it in the correct category. In turn, the players each scoot out and look for the correct food items to complete their food pyramid chart.

Only one food item can be returned per turn. Also, players have to return any food items they may already have on their chart.

Index

(alphabetical by game)

About the Author

Guy Bailey, M.Ed., has over 25 years of experience teaching physical education at the elementary and middle school levels, coaching youth sports, and directing after-school sport activities. His educational background includes having a B.S. degree (Central Washington University), and a M.Ed. degree (Portland State University) in his specialty area of physical education.

In addition to this book, Guy has authored three other popular books on physical education. *Recess Success!* is a special collection of 251 playground and recess activities for K-6 grade children. *The Physical Educator's Big Book of Sport Lead-Up Games* is a comprehensive resource of games used to develop sport skills, and has been adopted by many college professors throughout the country as a required text for their courses. *The Ultimate Homeschool Physical Education Game Book* is a unique collection of partner and small group games aimed at helping home educators teach physical education skills to children in the home and backyard setting.

Throughout his career as a physical educator, Guy's professional goal has been to equip each of his students with a love of movement and the basic skills needed to participate in an active lifestyle now and later as adults. He believes that for lasting skill learning to take place, physical education needs to consist of success-oriented learning experiences that literally leave children craving for more. This book reflects Guy's philosophy of using activities—both in the gymnasium and on the playground—that are not only skill based, but fun and meaningful as well.

In addition to his teaching and writing endeavors, Guy is actively involved in promoting literacy among elementary-age children. He has spoken at school assemblies on the subject of authoring books, and has worked with various community groups on motivating children to read more often.

Guy resides in Vancouver, Washington. He has three sons, Justin, Austin, Carson, and a daughter, Heather. In his spare time, he enjoys reading, writing, jogging, weightlifting, fishing, and hiking the various trails in the beautiful Columbia River Gorge near his home. He also has a passion for college athletics and is a frequent visitor to college stadiums and gymnasiums throughout the Pacific Northwest.

Guy is an active member of the American Alliance of Health, Physical Education, Recreation and Dance.

Ordering Information

Please contact your favorite educational catalog company or local bookstore to order additional copies of *Gym Scooter Fun & Games.* Customers can also order directly from Educators Press by using the contact information listed below. The retail cost is $15.95 per book plus $5.95 shipping (add $1 shipping for each additional book ordered). Washington state residents please add $1.29 per book for sales tax.

The following books are also available from Educators Press:

▶ **The Physical Educator's Big Book of Sport Lead-Up Games**
ISBN-10: 0966972759
ISBN-13: 978-0-9669727-5-7
$29.95 Retail Price

▶ **The Ultimate Homeschool Physical Education Game Book**
ISBN-10: 0966972740
ISBN-13: 978-0-9669727-4-0
$19.95 Retail Price

▶ **Recess Success!**
ISBN-13: 978-0-9669727-6-4
$21.95 Retail Price

Credit card purchases can be made through Educators Press by calling toll-free:

1-800-431-1579

All of our titles are available at special discounts for retailers, bookstores, distributors, sales promotions, and premium sale programs. For details, contact the sales manager at Educators Press by telephone at (360) 597-4355, fax (360) 326-1606, or by email at educatorspress@att.net.

EDUCATORS PRESS

15610 NE 2nd Street
Vancouver, WA 98684
(T) 360-597-4355   (F) 360-326-1606
www.educatorspress.com